COUNTRY AND MODERN

contemporary interiors for rural settings

DINAH HALL

QUADRILLE

CONTENTS

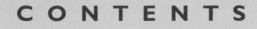

introduction 6

SIMPLICITY

spirit of country 10

pared down 32

ATTITUDE

retro version 54

new rustic 72

HONESTY

benign neglect 94

raw material 112

HARMONY

landscape and context 134

sources 154
architects and designers 157
picture credits/bibliography 158
index 159
acknowledgements 160

INTRODUCTION

'Country' is one of those words that have acquired an emotional skin around their literal meaning. It is more than a place, more than a picturesque address, more than a pretty patchwork of fields or a dramatic sweep of wilderness. Ever since a physical distinction could be made between rural and urban, 'Country' has represented a set of values, a way of thinking – and it has long contained alongside that notion the assumption of a kind of moral superiority over 'Town'. Centuries before the Industrial Revolution the countryside was viewed as an escape, both literally and metaphysically, from the city. And every age seems to feel the need to reinvent its own arcadia. Virgil turned the savage landscape of mythical Greece into a pastoral idyll; Wordsworth wrote passionately of the 'voice of Nature' shaping his life.

The romantic view of the countryside reached its apotheosis in nineteenth-century England, when it became fashionable to retire – but only temporarily, of course – from the artificial pleasures of town. In Regency England the wealthy retreated to what was, in effect, an equally artificial life – the *cottage orné*, where they could dabble for as long as it pleased them in a life of fashionable *faux*-poverty.

Since the early 1970s we have been busily reinventing our own versions of the *cottage orné*. Indulgence in a wealth of material possessions, together with an increasing awareness of the threats to the environment, resulted in Britain in the 'Colefax & Compost' lifestyle of the 1980s – no self-respecting hallway could be seen without its aesthetic displays of pretty straw hats, ostensibly for gardening in, and a line-up of green boots (unmuddied) was *de rigueur* in the grandest country house. But after a hard day's work tilling the compost you expected to be able to put your feet up in a cosy chintz drawing room, whose frills and furbelows were a remonstrance against the hard grind of modern life.

In the 'honest' Nineties, there has been a reaction against inappropriately opulent decoration. The lessons of history should teach us that our new, modest approach to simple interiors is as likely to contain a large pinch of artifice as any preceding style. (Clean lines invariably involve wads of filthy lucre, and is the 'urban peasant' who buys the Christian Liaigre look any different from the Regency fop who paid architects and upholsterers to create a rural pretence of unsophistication?) What distinguishes this new approach to country style is that modern design is no longer taboo: simplicity and sophistication are not necessarily a contradiction in terms.

SPIRIT OF COUNTRY

Like seals coming up for air, even the most committed urbanites need to take a break from city life occasionally to recharge their souls in the country. For others, living in the city is a necessary evil made bearable only by subscribing to the *rus in urbe* school of decoration – resulting sometimes in the rather sad spectacle of bizarrely inappropriate 'country kitchens' grafted onto modern town houses. Which only goes to show that 'country' is not something you can create out of a kit, using a paint by numbers mentality. It is not simply a material equation: wood + quarry tiles = country. Of course materials come into it, but the spirit of country goes deeper than surfaces and textures. Although this may sound worryingly ethereal to a generation raised on 'how to get the look' articles, the style (an uneasy word in this context, admittedly) consists largely of stripping down the layers of artifice that have been built up over years to reveal fundamental values – honesty of materials and simplicity in appearance. It is more to do with attitude than accumulation: recognizing that beauty does not always come with a price tag – that a stone found on the beach or a field of corn picked up in the colour of walls has far more value than the latest 'designer' accessories. True country interiors are not about surface decoration at all but rather the emotions which lie beneath surfaces and give them their structure.

'Honesty' is integral to the idea of country, which is why creating rustic escape hatches in the city ultimately does not work. Henry David Thoreau, the nineteenth-century American writer who lived the life of a semi-recluse for two years in a log cabin he built himself in the woods near Concord, Massachusetts, thought it was possible to bring country values to town. He claimed that 'the most interesting dwellings in this country ... are the most unpretending, humble log huts and cottages of the poor commonly; it is the life of the inhabitants whose shells they are, and not any peculiarity in their surfaces merely, which make them picturesque', and he didn't think you had to move out to the country or build a log cabin in town to create the same effect – the 'citizen's suburban box,' he declared, would be just as interesting 'when his life shall be as simple and as agreeable to the imagination, and there is as little straining after effect in the style of his dwelling.'

'Straining after effect' are the key words here – just as relevant, in fact far more so, after a century and a half of straining to the point of exhaustion in decorative terms. Houses that best convey the spirit of country are those in which you can relax. But let's be literally, as well as decoratively, honest here. We are talking about relaxing in calm spaces whose apparently effortless charms may well have required a considerable effort to achieve.

Design may move with the times (and we are more realistic about the picturesqueness of poverty than Thoreau) but the fundamental values which underpin living in the country do not change. Whether built of glass or stone, houses that cohabit, rather than compete, with the landscape are the ones that move the spirit. In 1941 Vita Sackville-West wrote that country houses which did not blend into their surroundings were those that were built 'to gratify the ostentation of some rich man in an age when display meant more than beauty; they were not allowed to grow with the oaks and elms and beeches; they were not true country houses at all, but a deliberate attempt to reproduce in the country the wealth and fame which their owner enjoyed in town. ' We could probably all think of similar examples today. Showing off may be tolerated in the city but somehow it offends natural laws in the country. In fact it probably obviates the whole point of living there for those who want to slow down the pace of life, to ground themselves.

We see the country as therapeutic, which is why, though we are happy to borrow the technological developments that have revolutionized the way we live, we still crave a simplicity of style, an aesthetic of reduction. It does not necessarily follow that these are budget interiors – but if a country interior is opulent, it is a quiet opulence: the equivalent of what the early twentieth-century French fashion designer Paul Poiret called *pauvreté de luxe*. This is very much a reaction to our times, which is why the words of architect-designer Owen Jones, written in 1856 in *The Grammar of Ornament*, at a time of similar rapid development, seem to have such resonance today. To 'return to a more healthy condition,' he wrote, 'we must even be as little children or as savages, we must get rid of the acquired and artificial, and return to and develop normal instincts.'

Traditionally, country interiors have leant heavily on the past. For most people the idea of 'modern' invading the countryside was pure heresy – even die-hard modernists in town seemed to come over all twee at the first whiff of manure. A change in this attitude is perhaps the most dramatic turning point in recent years – quite suddenly mixing modern and rural is no longer viewed as an unacceptable mingling of bloods. The spirit of country is at its most potent in a visually quiet interior that neither competes with nature, nor denies the present.

The spirit of country goes deeper

than surfaces and textures

New country style feeds off the past but doesn't devour it. In the clean, modern lines of a converted sheepfold the muted putty colour of an ornate antique French bed brings a breath of the past and yet retains total contemporary credibility. Above, the glamour of glitter and grit: an elegant chandelier hoist by rope is offset against the rugged utility of metal stairs and wooden walls.

'The soul of a house, the atmosphere of a house, are as much a part of the house as the architecture of that house or as the furnishings within it. Divorced from its life, it dies.'

VITA SACKVILLE-WEST

In this converted water tower in Belgium the wilder side of nature is reflected in the appropriately severe aesthetic of the interior. This is a home that confronts the world outside head on, rather than seeking refuge from it in a cosy cocoon of comfort, though it demands a level of exhibitionism — and tidiness — that would not suit everyone.

Beauty in the country does not come with a price tag: the appreciation of simple, wholesome foods and the transcendental joy of nature in close-up offer an approximation of spiritual bliss that it's hard to match in town.

Rural houses may borrow the best of **modern technology** for lighting and heating, but because the country is seen as an antidote to the stresses of city living we still crave a **simplicity of style**.

Rooms that on the surface may seem uncomfortably austere have a kind of **rhythm of life** that derives from the rough embrace of earthy materials, the collision of tradition with the unexpected — **sustenance for the soul** as well as the senses.

The appeal of the new rustic life lies not just in a picturesque fantasy of escapism but in a nostalgia for the days when man lived in harmony with nature.

The subliminal significance of a fire is far stronger than its physical presence – why else do we continue to build hearths in this age of central heating? Fire stokes up primeval emotions, particularly when contemplated from the womb-like comfort of a contemporary wing chair. Left, bare plaster walls demand strong art statements, like Robert Indiana's 'Eat Die'.

PARED DOWN

Minimalism has long been considered an urban conceit, as if only those living in town needed the spiritual uplift of a calm, uncluttered environment. Country interiors, as fed to us by countless books and magazines, were, on the other hand, not considered to be doing a proper job if there wasn't a dresser groaning with suitably rustic pottery and the beams didn't sport a healthy fungus of dried gypsophila, lavender and long-stemmed rosebuds. It was as if the inhabitants of these picturesque parlours needed to surround themselves with the perceived style, rather than the substance, of the country to convince themselves that they really belonged there.

Recently, however, the mood has shifted. People are keen to discard the artifice and superfluousness of stylized country interiors, realizing that a plethora of possessions actually creates barriers, that without them they have a healthier and more direct relationship with the countryside around them. Thoreau, who could be considered the godfather of today's minimalists — though admittedly he was rather more concerned with spiritual growth than whether his cabin would make it into the pages of *Architectural Digest* — wrote that 'before we can adorn our houses with beautiful objects the walls must be stripped and our lives must be stripped and beautiful living be laid for a foundation'. But of course you can take all this streamlining too far — Thoreau himself describes throwing out three pieces of limestone that, in a rare moment of frivolity, he had permitted himself as ornaments on his desk: he objected to the fact that they needed 'daily dusting when the furniture of my mind was all undusted still, and I threw them out the window in disgust.'

Agonizing over allowing yourself a few decorative or sentimental possessions should really be left to urban loft dwellers. Rural minimalism is an altogether more unselfconscious, relaxed affair that has its roots in history rather than style magazines. What could be more minimalist, after all, than the contemplative calm of a monastery, the severe lines of a medieval castle or the workmanlike beauty of a barn? Often the rooms that most move us in stately homes are not the glittering ballrooms and dressy drawing rooms, but the more utilitarian spaces like, for example, the kitchens of Edwin Lutyens's Castle Drogo in Devon, whose eloquent austerity has clear medieval references.

Paring down is not, however, just a matter of emptying a room of possessions. A place that has been simply stripped of its contents looks bare and depressing; it needs to have a strength and integrity of its own that resists embellishment. 'Let our houses first be lined with beauty,' wrote Thoreau, '... and not overlaid with it.' The reason we respond to the simple vernacular beauty of a log cabin or stone cottage is that they were built on the solid foundation of form, rather than the slippery slope of fashion or style. Their appeal is enduring, not tied to the dictates of fashion. As Stewart Brand, the American writer and inventor-designer, so neatly encapsulates it, 'Style is time's fool. Form is time's student.'

Reducing the clutter of furniture and objects does, however, allow you to appreciate the architecture of a room, while plain fabrics and materials are calming on the eye. But does this mean that we are denied the comfort that we tend to associate with country interiors? Not at all – though we might pause to consider that comfort is a spiritual as well as physical sensation. A spare environment intensifies the sensory delights of a fire – it puts us more in touch with elemental pleasures. And why upholster a room in floral chintzes when nature puts on a far superior show outside? The beauty of living close to nature is that you can be a temporary custodian of its surplus: a leaf, a bunch of wild flowers – these can be yours for a few days but the pleasure of owning them is essentially transient. Here possession is not bondage, as it is so often with 'precious' objects. This is partly why living in a holiday home has such a sense of freedom about it – it's not just because you are on holiday, it's because you are not burdened with belongings. Freed of clutter accumulated over a lifetime, the simple act of placing a jar of flowers on the table takes on an intensity of pleasure akin to a child's delight in such things: it's like the reawakening of a palate, jaded after years of over-indulgence.

Wood, preferably left untortured and as close to its primal condition as possible, remains an essential ingredient in the country house. But there are also man-made materials that have a kind of raw nobility to them – polished or resin-coated cement, for example, or concrete mixed with granite – or simply worked metals such as iron, steel and zinc. And there is nothing like a bit of brazen modernity to bring an old place alive.

Monastic simplicity sits better in the country than it does in town. What is the point, after all, of splashing your face with water in an elemental resin-coated cement bowl if you then have to submerge yourself in an underground train, jammed between others who clearly have not had such a positive experience with the wash-basin that morning? Left, conditioned as we are to equate country living with cosy comfort, severe beauty can seem quite shocking at first. Here the classic curves of an arch contrast with the startling insertion of a beech desk, designed by owner Greville Worthington 'after the style of Donald Judd', which also acts as a partition.

Stripped back interiors that could look arrogant in the town have a sense of **humility** in the country, as if paying homage to a superior designer. For who, when it comes down to it, can compete with nature's carpet of leaves?

Little wonder that today's minimalist designers so often look to ecclesiastical and monastic buildings for inspiration. In spaces once used to glorify God, the space itself is now worshipped for its calm and contemplative aura. In this converted Yorkshire chapel the owners have sensibly accentuated its simple eloquence rather than been tempted by the other possible route of Gothic grandiloquence. Whisper-thin muslin filters the light and allows the windows to figure without completely dominating the room, while the skeletal elegance of the Arne Jacobsen chairs are a perfect foil to the solid masonry of the space. If proof were needed that contemporary and previous styles complement each other, this is it – a hymn to ancient and modern.

Comfort is a spiritual as

well as physical sensation

'Let our houses first be lined with beauty
... and not overlaid with it.'

HENRY DAVID THOREAU

'It is alien to the nature of an Englishman of standing to envelope himself in luxury,' commented Hermann Muthesius, a German architect and observer of English design at the beginning of the twentieth century. Other visitors to Britain – Americans in particular – were never quite so enamoured of having to pad across freezing cold linoleum floors in the middle of the night in the name of 'country house tradition'. But maybe Muthesius had a point. Certainly the trend in recent years to make the most of huge country bathrooms by turning them into upstairs sitting rooms complete with chintz armchairs and overblown curtains went a little too far the other way. This rather spartan-looking bathroom may invoke that more distant 'invigorating cold bath' school of country-house design, but it is in keeping with the concept of *pauvreté de luxe* – the shower is hidden behind the wall and the bath is cedarwood.

The simple, pared-down rural interior is softer and less self-conscious than its urban cousin. Far from being a refugee style from the city, it is a look that has its roots in medieval simplicity – the spare beauty of castles and monasteries, the cathedral-like grace of barns.

Where there is a powerful relationship
between a house and the land it sits in,
interior decoration seems extraneous.
Who needs paintings on the wall, when you have a
tantalizing fragment of view, framed by a window or door?

R E T R O V E R S I O N

Over the last two centuries, nostalgia has provided a comfortably padded
background for country life. But whether it was the Georgians creating a
rustic fantasy or urban weekend escapees in the 1980s reacting against their
high tech lives in the city with faded chintz and wicker baskets, the imagery
that they played with had to be suitably distant from their own times, and
had to be securely compartmentalized from city life. If you had a stainless
steel kitchen in your city apartment, then you had to have a rustic wood one
in the country; if your urban furniture was the latest slick Italian job, in the
country you sank gratefully into the familiar embrace of a battered old
armchair that had done the rounds in your extended family.

Today, however, the design barriers between urban and rural are dissolving – as is the cut-off point in nostalgia. The Sixties and Seventies are still regarded as a definite minority taste, even in city interiors, so for them to have found their way into rural habitats seems quite breathtakingly audacious. Curiously, thirty-year-old 'modernity' is regarded as more challenging in this context than the most up to date contemporary (possibly because the design of that era was so strongly associated with urban hedonism – as if you weren't allowed a bit of wild fun in the country!). In fact, placed in an unexpected situation this style can actually come to life, revealing in its organic forms and sweeping curves a relationship to nature that makes you wonder if its real home wasn't the country after all.

Of course, this does depend on situation. Bean bags and lava lamps are probably not going to look their best mixed with reproduction eighteenth-century furniture in a beamed cottage with thatched roof. And we can't ignore the power of fashion – our resistance to a new or 'reassessed' style is worn down by constant exposure to it. Just as you may have sworn you would never be seen dead in a 1960s geometric shirt and then found yourself lusting after one three months later, so painful associations with 1970s furniture will fade away.

For British interior designer Philip Hooper furnishings were dictated by where he lives. We've all played that game on holiday where you 'adopt' a certain house, fantasize about it being yours. Hooper had long admired a 1950s house built on stilts along a stretch of the East Sussex coastline. It had belonged to the same family since it was built in 1958 and such was its unique character and position that should it ever come on the market it would be extremely unlikely to stay there for long. When it was eventually put up for sale, friends who lived locally tipped Hooper off: he immediately sold his flat in London and set about raising enough money to buy the coastal property. Given that his work was in London, this was a fairly impractical thing to do but then a house like this only comes along once in a lifetime.

Inside the fittings were all authentic – it had always been used as a family holiday house so they were fairly basic but integral to the design of the whole. Kitchen cupboards are raised on brackets above the stairwell leading down to the bedroom floor, while a glass cupboard suspended by metal straps in mid-air gives a sense of division between the living and cooking area. Even some of the furniture that Hooper inherited with the house was original. The long wooden table, though it may look nothing out of the ordinary, was designed specially for the house at the time by a young unknown called Terence Conran... As a designer it must have been very tempting for Hooper to make his own statement here – to wipe out the past and let his ego off the leash. To his credit, he could not bring himself to demolish the spirit of the place. Instead, working from the given style, he gradually built up a collection of choice British and European period pieces. He has not, though, by any means locked himself in the past and thrown away the key. The white grid bookcase with rounded corners and orange interiors is his own design and fits in perfectly. And as a concession to comfort he also added a modern Danish wood-burning stove, placing it unconventionally in front of the glass doors to make the most of the sea view.

Those less devoted to design history may well find the more homely 'new utilitarian' style, reminiscent of the 1940s, easier to relate to a country setting. Although the original utility concept stemmed from the austerity of the war and postwar years, this is not just a nostalgic retake – a kind of stylized impoverishment. New utility in the country celebrates the comfort of simple shapes and modest design: black and white used together have an elemental freshness that is completely different from the hard-edged flashiness of urban monochrome. Inspiration also comes from the most utilitarian of fabrics – tea towels, old mattress tickings, even floor cloths have become (quite inexplicably to those of an earlier generation who knew them only too intimately in another context) sought after for the wholesomeness of their design.

Ground rules about what constitutes a suitably rustic style are constantly being eroded. It is no longer an offence to be found not in possession of an Aga and a

dresserful of naive rustic pottery in the country. Nor is nostalgia limited to previous centuries. The only style that is not comfortable is the one that is foisted upon you.

It would have been easy
to create a fashionably
minimalist haven in this
seaside house so destroying
its integrity. Instead Philip
Hooper pursued the lead
suggested by its authentic
1958 interior and furnished
it with classics of the period,
like the Poole pottery,
Venini glass and Robin Day
armchairs. The table is an
early Conran design made
for the house; the bookcase
is by Hooper.

The Chelsea living room of octogenarian furniture designer Robin Day and his textile designer wife Lucienne could easily be mistaken for a contemporary country interior. In fact the room has barely changed in forty years – it's just that the rest of the world has finally caught up with the Days and their respect for simple, pure materials and modern design with soul.

French designer Christian Liaigre's island holiday home in Brittany is stripped back to a bare, but not severe, aesthetic that celebrates the uncomplicated pleasures of vacation life. To over-indulge in luxury and all mod. cons would be entirely inappropriate for the situation – 'We don't pretend to be a four-star hotel here. We're a holiday house and to hell with comfort.' It is not, of course, without style, though it is a style rooted in vernacular tradition. The immaculate matchboarding of the walls, for example, echoes the local practice of panelling interiors as a precaution against damp. Before this elegantly austere background, Liaigre's signature dark furniture – designed specifically for the house – stands out in bold contrast.

It could only happen in a post-feminist era – a yearning for the **gadget-free simplicity** of the 1940s kitchen when women wore pinnies and baked apple pie. Certainly you have to be suitably distanced from a working relationship with the tea towel or floor cloth to see the **design potential** in its colour and pattern.

'Home is about the familiar, about gravity, about falling back into the self after being dispersed and overextended in the world.'

STEWART BRAND

If you grew up in the 1960s, you are more likely to associate that era with the comfort and security of childhood than with its surface style and legendary excitement. The owners of this 1963 Long Island ranch were keen to keep the spirit of the place, rather than sink it under a Nineties façade. They have amassed a good collection of mid-century modern, including the Robsjohn Gibbings sofa and table, and Bertoia chairs.

The Renaissance origins
of this Italian jewellery
designer's country house
have not been allowed
to overawe the contents.
Instead she has raided
different eras with the
alacrity of a child at
the pick'n'mix counter –
using the monastic
sobriety of bare plaster
walls as a foil for
startling combinations
of colour and
curvaceous shapes.

NEW RUSTIC

Deep within each one of us lies the spirit of a primitive hut dweller. In most of us it's tucked away as a half-forgotten childhood memory, startled to life by a passing moment as mundane as the whiff of sun on creosote some hot summer afternoon. Remember the childish thrill of making a home in the garden shed, taking pretend tea from crockery smuggled from the kitchen while sitting cross legged on a pile of itchy potato sacks? We may grow up to live in suburban comfort or the gritty glamour of an inner city loft, but nothing ever again seems to quite compare with that early satisfaction of makeshift homemaking, creating a rugged simplicity that was entirely your own.

Inevitably, perhaps, the incredibly rich selection of fabrics, furniture, paints and accessories that has flooded the market in recent years has resulted in decorating overload, decision breakdown. Like the over-indulged gourmet craving the simplicity of a boiled egg, more people are seeking to build, from choice rather than necessity, homes with a kind of savage beauty that refer back to a pioneering spirit yet have a strangely futuristic edge to them.

Where once the dream country home may have conjured up visions of thatched cottages or mellow stone barns, there is now a new definition of beauty. And it is the antithesis of quaint. Of course this has happened in the city too, with the colonizing of industrial buildings – not just the architecturally picturesque nineteenth-century lofts but also more 'difficult' 1960s office blocks as the shortage of what are generally considered aesthetically pleasing buildings left to convert forces us to revise our judgement. In a wilderness landscape the rawness of more recent farm outbuildings with their palette of concrete and corrugated iron can be as powerful as the beams and stone of centuries-old barns. New-built houses may play with the rustic ideal, referring back to Scandinavian/New England roots in their use of wood, but they have an unadorned rigour that links them back to the mythical hut while using thoroughly contemporary language.

'We're all, to a degree, looking for childhood memories of home,' believes Neil Winder, an English architect who has built a modern, eco-friendly house with definite elements of what he calls 'shackology'. Despite having worked for such aggressively contemporary architects as Norman Foster and Richard Rogers in the past, he has reverted to an outwardly traditional style of building in his own home – probably because of childhood associations with security. 'It's reassuring to have certain images, materials. Like timber, for example. We feel reassured by it – maybe it is a feeling that goes back to your childhood, but it could be that it goes deeper than that – maybe it goes back generations.'

For Winder – imbued with the pioneer spirit after weeks of backbreaking work, pulling up large areas of thicket and nettles – it felt right to use local timbers, even though that meant buying unseasoned wood. There is a huge snobbery about timber – a softwood like larch is seen as only fit for fencing. But Winder liked the rough-hewn quality of it and wanted to use it for weatherboarding and the decking of the verandah: 'Yes, it may rot – but probably not before I die. Personally I think there's a lot of mythology around the issue of untreated timber – nobody's really tried it, and I think I have developed an understanding of how to use it.' And of course the satisfaction of seeing trees growing in a forest, then arriving on a lorry as cut wood a week later and in another few months seeing them standing in place as walls can not be compared to the humdrum business of buying precut batches of timber off the shelf at the local builders' merchant. One is pure romance, the other computer dating.

The urge to return to a simpler lifestyle, more in tune with the rhythm of nature, coincides with a global need to consider the environment. The appeal of 'shackology' lies not just in a picturesque fantasy of escapism but a nostalgia for the days when we lived, if not exactly in symbiosis with nature, then at least in a benign mastery of it. New housing developments in town are often built with a nod towards conservation – perhaps in a more efficient use of energy – but, because of the closer proximity to nature, it is somehow even more obscene to build a new country house without an ecological agenda. Neil Winder has gone further than most, in creating a home built to withstand future climactic changes connected with global warming. The composting toilet may require a change in habits that only the most dedicated few will be prepared to make, but using non-toxic paints, preservatives, glues and resins is easily within the bounds of possibility, as is the notion of raising buildings above the ground to allow underbuilding air circulation. Winder's central heating, hot water and an oven are all supplied by a modern version of the ceramic tile stove once common in Scandinavia and Russia. Using local coppiced timber for fuel, it needs to burn for only an hour in the morning and an hour in the afternoon to provide heat for four rooms over twenty-four hours. The more sophisticated we become as a society, the more it seems that for contemporary ecological solutions we need to look back and learn from the past.

We are learning to reassess what is beautiful — for the
new country **pioneers** the rugged nobility of a
hardworking modern farm outbuilding with **no frills**
has more romance to it than a chocolate-box thatched cottage.

No matter how many **technologically advanced** materials we are capable of inventing, somehow we always return to tried and tested forms of construction. A newly built adobe follows traditional methods of building with its walls of mud, sand and straw but this does not proscribe a modern life within.

'Houses are the domain of slowly shifting fantasies and rapidly shifting needs.'

STEWART BRAND

The owners of this
converted tractor barn
in Australia responded
to its raw industrial/
agricultural aesthetic by
'foraging' for furnishings.
The barn had literally
been built from the mud
it stood upon and so
it seemed appropriate
to source what they
needed from local
shops, markets and
other people's rejects,
rather than importing
city affluence. The tin
bath, originally used by
a caterer for washing
vegetables, was found
abandoned on the side
of a road. It may not be
luxurious, but it suits
the pioneer spirit of
the building.

In the country you can take
inspiration from nature,
the greatest decorator of all; better
still if you can blur the boundaries
between inside and out and
**borrow from the
landscape.**

The raw sensuality of stripped-back materials – brick, corrugated iron and wood – has a surprising power in this South African home built around a stable: instead of competing with the landscape as a more 'decorative' look might, it complements it. Buildings like this, whose strength lies in their relationship with their surroundings, lend themselves to a more casual style of furnishing, almost as if the owner were just a temporary custodian (think camping in, not camping up). Curtains or blinds would domesticate the space and tip the finely tuned balance it enjoys between living in the wild and civilization too far towards polite society.

Borrowing texture and robustness from the landscape it inhabits, **contemporary rustic** has a kind of **wholesome sophistication**.

New rustic houses
may contain echoes
of the past – indeed
references to traditional
imagery may serve a
psychic need in us to be
connected to that past ...

... but they are also solidly grounded in **contemporary** thinking.

ONESTY

BENIGN NEGLECT

Contrary though it may seem, leaving an old building as it is instead of rushing to restore or convert sometimes has a modern sensibility to it. There is a subtle difference, though, between this and the careful pickling of country interiors in fussy nostalgia.

Christopher Alexander, the American architect and theorist, believes that 'buildings are like people – not impervious and alien, but alive, changing with time, remembering the paths which people tread. Revealing the archaeological layering of a house – allowing the past to breathe, rather than stifling it in some kind of Disneyesque caricature of olde worlde charm – is a way of giving context to the contemporary. This is why the most successful re-use of old buildings is in the conversions which acknowledge and respect their previous existence without slavishly reproducing past style: it may be something as simple as leaving areas of the original structure or decoration exposed. Buildings which have had all traces of their industrial or agricultural heritage wiped out – ancient barns condemned to a suburban existence, for example, with plastered walls and pinch-pleat curtains – lose any sense of integrity.

Buildings, we have come to realize, are much more than just a structure – they shelter dreams as well as people. Stewart Brand expands on this perception when he explains that to 'tinker with a house is to commune with the people who have lived in it before and to leave messages for those who will live in it later. Every house is a living museum of habitation, and a monument to all the lives and aspirations that have flickered within it.'

Sometimes, in our haste to stamp our own personality on a house, we extinguish all those flickering lives and aspirations and in doing so create what feels like a one-dimensional home. Equally, though, it is a mistake not to touch a house with our own lives, to find ourselves through a lack of confidence inhabiting a kind of historical stage set, where modern appliances appear as unscripted intruders.

Rupert Spira, an English potter who makes beautifully spare, elemental hand-thrown earthenware, lives in a way that on the surface might appear nostalgic in a house that seems barely touched by the present. But he refutes this perception entirely: 'It would be impossible to live if you were trying to recreate a rustic ideal from the past. The countryside exists now just as much as in the past, and I don't feel at odds in any way with contemporary culture and modern habits. I hate this idea that unless you're living in town you're hardly human.' It may look as if he and his wife have simply slapped a preservation order on the rooms of their sixteenth-century farmhouse, with its extraordinary nineteenth-century stencilled bedroom left almost intact, but it's more complicated than that. Walls and floors are left bare largely because they enjoy materials in their raw state 'It's the same kind of aesthetic that is in my pots – in general, I ask, "What can I take away?" rather than "What can I add?"' He had no intention of creating a house with a period feel, however, and decisions he has taken have nothing to do with preservation, conservation or looking back. 'I like raw materials – stone, wood, glass, clay, lime paint – not because of what they represent but for the qualities they share: simplicity, elegance, unpretentiousness, a lack of complication.' Whether something is old or modern is irrelevant – the halogen lights in the kitchen, he points out, have the same characteristics as the hundred-year-old plank of wood they shine on, which now functions as a table. They are both elegant, made of fine materials and, most important of all, serve their purpose well.

In one room, however, Spira does admit that he and his wife have been perhaps overawed by history, and it does present a moral dilemma. In many of the rooms layers of original paint or plaster blend with areas of their own experimentation and the result is almost poetical in its intensity, leaving you hard put to decide whether the effect is intentional or haphazard. But in this one bedroom the walls, untouched for over 150 years, are covered in what looks like very old wallpaper but is actually original stencilling The fact that it has survived so long untouched and that it is unique of its kind were enough to persuade them to keep it but the truth is that the room is dingy and an unpleasant place to sleep. Sentiment aside, he knows that what it needs to liberate it from museum status to a living, breathing room is a good coat of lime paint. But who dares slap on the first brushful?

Knowing when to leave well alone is an art in itself, perhaps even more intellectually demanding than designing from scratch: it is certainly not a lazy option.

CH CH AS
CH CH AS

Leave at least one element
untouched – it is like a
calling card from the past.

Allowing the past to breathe is quite different from the inherent falsehood of deliberately re-creating the past. It provides **context for the contemporary**, encouraging us to choose only those objects that have the strength and integrity to live with what has gone before.

A considered decision to
leave a place as you find it –
as opposed to being too lazy to lift a
paintbrush – is a contemporary tribute
to the **past life of a building.**

'A house that has been experienced is not an inert box.'

GASTON BACHELARD

On the face of it
you couldn't get much
less modern than this
bedroom in a Shropshire
farmhouse. The walls
were stencilled in
1830 and, amazingly,
left untouched ever
since. Though previous
occupants were probably
mucking out cowsheds
rather than making
design statements in
their own neglect of
it, in Rupert Spira's
custody it could
almost be a
contemporary
art installation.

'Every house is a work in progress.... It begins in the imagination of the people who build it and is gradually transformed, for better and for worse, by the people who occupy it down through the years, decades, centuries.'

STEWART BRAND

Benign neglect may well involve preserving not so much the physicality as the spirit of the past – but this does not mean looking upon contemporary design as a rude intruder.

R A W
M A T E R I A L

Vernacular buildings have a timelessness and universal appeal precisely because they grew out of a solid connection with nature and their environment – they were built using materials that were to hand. But there is a danger that we venerate these kinds of buildings at the expense of growth. As Steward Brand has illustrated in his book *How Buildings Learn*, there is also something profoundly moving about a house that tells a continuing story in the additions that have been made over the years.

This is not to say that materials which have stood the test of time should as a matter of principle be ousted in favour of the new, just that we should remain open to fresh possibilities. Concrete, for example, once loved only by brutalist architects and pavement builders but now enjoying an avant-garde renaissance, is unlikely to have a place in a centuries-old stone cottage. For many people its associations with dank, dubious smells in the stairwells of multi-storey car-parks will never be overcome. In a barn conversion, however, its tough, contemporary language may converse with the original, workmanlike structure more fluently than more 'domestic' materials, though there is a case to be made for limiting its use – if only for the sake of future generations. Concrete doesn't crumble aesthetically in environmentally friendly fashion, and it is not easy to adapt to different needs and designs. Also it does not have what Stewart Brand calls the quality of 'forgivingness' that we respond to in materials like stone and brick which have aged well over centuries. But worst of all, it currently wears a fashion label. And while fashion may be fun for architects to play with, points out Brand, it is a poisonous legacy for building users: 'When the height of fashion moves on, they're the ones left behind, stuck in a building that was designed to look good rather than work well, and now it doesn't even look good.'

The materials you use should work with, rather than camouflage, the house's structure. In an old converted building, exposing brickwork rather than plastering over all the walls acknowledges and expresses the existence of a previous life. We rarely consciously analyse what it is about age-old materials like wood, brick and stone that makes us respond so positively to them. Why is it, for example, that a modern brick-built house can leave us emotionally cold, while we warm to the sight of brick that has mellowed over the years? Wordsworth believed stone cottages 'remind the spectator of a production of nature and rather may be said to have grown than to have been created, to have risen, by instinct of their own, out of naked rock'. But in some way we also feel linked through these materials to past lives. 'Time finds its way into our buildings, working somewhere beneath the consciousness of architects and builders and inhabitants, but shaping our dreams of place all the same,' writes

Michael Pollan in his extraordinary book *A Place of My Own* – part romance, part DIY guide – about the making of a small wooden 'writing cabin' in the woods behind his house.

In the process of choosing different woods for his house and furniture he came to understand the nature of wood and our relationship with it. Different woods, he realized, carry an extraordinary amount of 'cultural' baggage with them, so 'selecting a wood for an interior means weighing not only the species, appearance and material qualities, but also the history of its use and whatever architectural fashions have imprinted themselves on it....' Maple, for example, is forever wedded to Danish Modern, while because of its links with Arts & Crafts he finds oak 'almost too woody a wood'. All the libraries and studies panelled in wood, he suggests, have as their ancestor the Renaissance *studiolo* and 'the scent of masculinity given off by rooms panelled in dark wood ... has its source in the exclusively male preserve of the study'. Thus are our spaces 'wedded ineluctably to our history, to times that, though we may have long ago forgotten, our buildings nonetheless remember'.

Soft furnishings, being so much more transitory, are inevitably more vulnerable to fashion trends but it is still possible to apply the same kind of criteria to choosing fabrics as you would to the more solid elements of a house. Certain materials age well, softening with use and somehow sitting more happily than others in a country environment. Linen and leather might almost be considered blood relations of wood and stone in this respect, though you may think the current trend for buying expensive 'antique' linen sheets – i.e. slept in by someone else before you – is taking things a bit far, even if that someone else was a nineteenth-century French peasant (somehow 'English peasant' never sounds quite as desirable as French peasant, does it?). Utility fabrics like ticking and artists' linen have a freshness that never dates, and they are ideally suited to country interiors – in town their very modesty can look a little contrived and self-conscious.

The stark beauty of a stone wall needs no enhancing, but demands equal visual integrity from what is put before it – the raw appeal of timber, the pure form of earthenware.

Stone has a strength beyond its sheer physical carrying properties. Its raw, elemental nature connects us back to the earth, while in its natural attrition we can find tactile comfort in the passing of time.

Leather and linen – the spiritual cousins of wood and stone

Country living does not
have to be a soft option —
concrete and metal have
raw, unrefined qualities
that sit well with the
wildness of nature.

Our emotional attachment to mellow, time-worn materials should not blinker us to the possibilities of marrying old and new in a dazzling alliance.

Ecological guilt has given us a greater appreciation of softwoods once thought fit only for garden sheds and fences; in fact their workmanlike quality fits into a country setting far better than more exotic woods. In this Suffolk house the verandah deck and weatherboarding were made from unseasoned larch, the raw, rough-hewn quality of which was preserved by treating it only with a natural, oil-based, micro-porous paint which soaks into the timber without camouflaging it.

Left, a chorus line of doors reveals how even the thinnest veneers and most basic of woods have a natural beauty. Right, in a converted Yorkshire chapel a selection of materials from natural to man-made work together in perfect harmony. Woods are easy to use because they rarely clash, even if they differ dramatically in tone and quality. An elegant modern beech daybed and table, framed by the quiet splendour of old stone walls, are perfectly at home with the solid lines of an old timber table, which in turn gives dramatic contrast to the machine aesthetic of the Arne Jacobsen chair.

Houses built from locally available materials, proven to age attractively, have a given aesthetic, an inbuilt sense of belonging – they can never look out of place.

'Though the tree stops growing when it's cut, it doesn't stop developing and changing. "Acquiring character" is what we say it's doing, as a wood surface absorbs our oils and accumulates layers of grime, as it is dignified by use and time.'

MICHAEL POLLAN

LANDSCAPE
AND CONTEXT

In the city we tend to turn our backs on our surroundings, retreating snail-like into our own private shells: the outside world, often viewed as ugly and threatening, is kept at bay. In the country, conversely, houses have a vested interest in the environment: the view outside becomes part of the interior landscape, so that we tend to feel more 'connected' in a country home.

The siting of a house in a landscape is of fundamental importance. Writer Michael Pollan spent days walking around his land trying to find the perfect location for his little wooden cabin. 'Some sites I considered offered what seemed like the geographical correlative of shyness, others self-assertion. It was as though the landscape were asking me to declare myself, to say this place, and not that one, suited me, in some sense *was* me.' And when he had at last completed his project, he knew he had chosen well for 'my building seemed a welcome addition to the landscape – this warm-looking, wide-awake envelope of light set down in the middle of the darkening woods ... seemed to order the shadowy rocks and trees all around it, to wrest a bright space of habitation from the old, indifferent darkness.'

Though from widely differing social and cultural backgrounds Vita Sackville-West, born in an imposing English stately home, and Frank Lloyd Wright, native of Wisconsin, both saw the need for architecture that was integral to landscape. Sackville-West wrote that 'the house is essentially part of the country, not only *in* the country, but part of it, a natural growth. Irrespective of grandeur or modesty, it should agree with its landscape,' while the architect of the Prairie Houses declared that 'no house should ever be *on* a hill or *on* anything. It should be *of* the hill. Belonging to it....'

But living in harmony with the landscape is not an uncomplicated choice. There are two opposing forces at work in the construction of human habitation – an instinctive desire for shelter against the elements and the conflicting desire to commune with them. In European houses the former has perhaps been the more dominant force while Americans have tended to share Thoreau's view that 'in wilderness is the preservation of the world'. American houses, exemplified by Lloyd Wright's designs, somehow have a much more thrusting relationship to the landscape.

Windows have a crucial role to play as intermediaries between inside and out. In old houses, they tended to be made very small to preserve warmth in winter (and in any case, as Michael Pollan points out, before the nineteenth century when the Romantics made a virtue of the landscape, people preferred to hide from the view and its potential terrors: it was enough to know there were grizzly bears out there without looking at them). So there was a kind of knee-jerk reaction when it came to building modern houses in the era of central heating. In celebration of the fact that we were no longer constrained by practicalities, enormous picture windows trained their glassy eyes on the seascape and countryside, hogging the view like ugly architectural cyclopses. In fact, huge, all-embracing windows are not always the solution they seem to be. Far from putting us closer in touch with nature, Chris Alexander argues, they may actually alienate us from the view. A window should increase the intensity with which we view something. Small, narrow windows achieve this by giving different perspectives depending on where you are standing in a room, increasing the sense of intimacy, whereas one large window allows you to see everything at once and offers no surprises. There is also the fact that a plate glass window cuts out the other senses that support the visual pleasure of looking at a landscape: as Michael Pollan points out without the 'additional information provided by the senses of smell and touch and hearing, the world as perceived through a plate of glass can seem profoundly, and disconcertingly, inaccessible'. He recalls the seaside house his family had when he was a child. Its front wall, which looked out on to the sea, was almost entirely glazed but far from putting him in closer touch with the environment, it made a couch potato of him. The picture window had turned nature into a 'spectator sport'.

Less obvious but almost as significant as the window in the relationship between inside and out is boundary space. Whether it takes the form of verandah, terrace or a more basic demarcation of territory, houses that seem to have a special relationship with the landscape often have some kind of bridging space between the front door and the great outdoors. Even if it is only a fairly superficial kind of demarcation – a path of brick or stone, say – it somehow eases the transition from inside to out. Verandahs and terraces have the added bonus of providing a sense of 'indoors' outside, but without them it is still possible, and desirable, to create makeshift shelters that give the same satisfaction. A simple fabric construction – a sheet tethered between trees – is just as effective (and arguably more appropriate in the country than a parasol). In it is echoed not only the happy memories of childhood dens created out of chair legs and blankets, but also the mythical beginnings of the primitive hut, when four trees interleaved their branches overhead to create shelter for Man.

An obsession with views is a relatively modern phenomenon. The slit window in the bathroom of this Majorcan house designed by architect Claudio Silvestrin is a purely practical solution, based on an age-old local tradition, but in a modern house it can not help but project a more abstract significance. The plate-glass window was modernism's greatest ego trip: it announced not only that we had insulated ourselves from the vagaries of climate but it also allowed us to believe that in some way we possessed what the eye could see. Left, it is awe inspiring to be able to open up to the landscape, as in this modern New Mexican adobe, but the view might lose its impact if it was constantly available.

'In wilderness is the salvation of the world.'

HENRY DAVID THOREAU

Built of timber and rough-hewn tree trunks, this house on Stradbroke Island off south-eastern Queensland in Australia gives the impression of having grown naturally out of its environment. Perching above the trees, it gives a perfect view of migrating whales on the ocean.

'we humans are never simply in nature, like the beasts and trees and boulders, but are always also *in relation* to nature: looking at it through the frames of our various preconceptions, our personal and collective histories, our self-consciousness, our words'

MICHAEL POLLAN

Restrictive planning regulations in Britain mean that few innovative country houses ever get beyond the drawing board. Baggy House in Devon is one exception. The cliff-top house is an architectural symphony of modern mechanics and natural materials. Windows wind right down into the ground to leave rooms entirely open to the elements. Limestone floors are cool on hot days yet, with underfloor heating, warm underfoot in winter. The use of indigenous materials like granite and slate gives the house local context, but the architect Anthony Hudson has not been restricted by tradition: ceilings are clad in verdigrised copper, and elsewhere in lead. References to the maritime surroundings can be seen in the rope and zinc-sprayed steel balustrading.

The way the inside **connects** to the outside affects
our **sense of well-being**. A verandah, planting or steps
softens the boundaries, while even the most primitive canopy
extends the **concept of shelter** outside.

Glass allows us both shelter and
participation in the landscape.

'Nature in our daily life should be thought

of as part of the biological need.' CHRISTOPHER ALEXANDER

SOURCES

accessories

CUCINA DIRECT
PO Box 6611, London SW15 2WG, tel 0870 420 4300
www.cucinadirect.co.uk
Pretty blue chintz pudding bowls, enamel bread bins, pastel enamel utilityware as well as kitchen classics

MINT
70 Wigmore Street, London WIU 2SF, tel 020 7224 4406
www.mintshop.co.uk
Distinctive modern design – quirky and original objects and furniture

EVERTRADING BY MAIL
Unit 3 New Rock Industrial Estate, Chilcompton, Radstock BA3 4JE, tel 0845 130 6725
www.evertrading.co.uk
Beautiful glassware, cushions and other well-sourced accessories - elegant and contemporary, with a romantic twist. Occasional furniture too, like the wonderful sheepskin covered armchair

CABANE
IA 4 Third Avenue, Hove BN3 2PD, tel 0870 242 7619
www.cabane.co.uk
Capsule collection of simple French style – lambs wool throws, blankets, kitchen linens and home accessories by mail order

THE HOUSE OF EROJU
4 Burke House, Hope Street Battersea, London SW11 2BY
tel 020 7738 9374
Info@houseoferoju.com
www.houseoferoju.com
Door handles and pulls in stainless steel and leather

TWELVE
19 Barn Street, London N16 0JT, tel 020 7812 9700
Twelve@massn16.co.uk
www.twelvelimited.com
Simple, chunky furniture and accessories, such as oak book magazine and blocks, made from natural or recycled materials

DAVID MELLOR
4 Sloane Square, London SW1W 8EE, tel 020 7730 4259
www.davidmellordesign.com
Unerringly well-designed kitchen and dining equipment

MELIN TREGWYNT
Tregwynt Mill, Castlemorris Haverfordwest, Pembrokeshire SA62 5UX, tel 01348 891644
www.melintregwynt.co.uk
Blankets, cushions and throws in wide spectrum of colours, woven in family mill

TOAST
D Ashmount Park, Upper Fforest Way, Llansamlet Swansea SA6 8QR
tel 0870 240 5200
www.toastbypost.co.uk
Primarily a fashion catalogue, Toast also do the best linen sheets and duvet covers plus occasional home accessories like hunks of quality soap and beeswax candles

RUPERT SPIRA
Church Farm, More, Bishops Castle, Shropshire SY9 5HH
tel 01588 650588
www.rupertspira
Potter Rupert Spira's studio is open strictly by appointment only

STEPAN TERTSAKIAN
Prince Rupert House, 64 Queen Street London EC4R IAD
tel 020 7236 8788
www.stertsakiansheepskins.co.uk
john@stertsakiansheepskins.co.uk
Sheepskin rugs and other skins for interior use

CARDEN CUNIETTI
81-83 Westbourne Park Road London W2 5QH
tel 020 7229 8630
www.carden-cunietti.com
Eclectic glamorous mix of period and modern

furniture

FEATHER & BLACK
Terminus Road, Chichester West Sussex PO19 8ZZ
tel 01243 380 600
www.featherandblack.com
Large choice of beds from classic ornate iron and French empire to contemporary minimal fourposters, New England simplicity and leather beds. Also coordinating furniture plus mattresses and bed linen. Branches nationwide

WILLIAM GARVEY
Leyhill, Payhembury, Honiton Devon EX14 3JG
tel 01404 841430
www.williamgarvey.co.uk
Furniture designers and makers who specialise in exquisitely simple teak baths, basins and kitchen sinks. Special sizes made to order

SKANDIUM
86 Marylebone High Street London WIU 4QS
tel 020 7935 2077
www.skandium.com
Contemporary and classic Scandinavian design

B&B ITALIA
250 Brompton Road, London SW3 2AS, tel 020 7591 8111
www.bebitalia.it
The ultimate Italian sofas and chairs

ISOKON
Turnham Green Terrace Mews London W4 IQU
tel 020 8994
www.isokonplus.com

...bookshelves and coffee tables in birch or walnut – modern but with a retro twist. Plus classic designs by Eames, Breuer etc.

SCP

135-39 Curtain Road, London
EC2A 3DX, tel 020 7739 1869
www.scp.co.uk
Strong modern furniture design without frills or gimmicks

VIADUCT

1-10 Summers Street, London
EC1R 5BD, tel 020 7278 8456
www.viaduct.co.uk
Comprehensive collection of European contemporary furniture

INHOUSE

28 Howe Street, Edinburgh
EH3 6TG, tel 0131 225 2888
www.inhousenet.co.uk
Long established source of the best in contemporary design

eco-products

SECOND NATURE UK LTD

Soulands Gate, Dacre, Penrith
Cumbria CA11 0JF
tel 017684 86285
www.secondnatureuk.com
Sheeps wool insulation for roofs

AURO ORGANIC PAINTS

Cheltenham Road, Bisley,
Stroud, Gloucestershire GL6

7BX, tel 01452 772020
www.auro.co.uk
Natural paints, varnishes and wood stains

THE CENTRE FOR ALTERNATIVE TECHNOLOGY

Machynlleth, Powys SY20 9AZ
tel 01654 702400
www.cat.org.uk
Environmental charity aiming to 'inspire, inform, and enable' people to live more sustainably. Courses in ecological and sustainable building techniques.

THE HEALTHY HOUSE

The Old Co-Op, Lower Street
Ruscombe, Stroud
Gloucestershire GL6 6BU
tel 01453 752216
www.healthy-house.co.uk
Bedding, paints, and domestic products for allergen-free households

NUTSHELL NATURAL PAINTS

PO Box 72, South Brent TQ10
9YR, tel 00708 331140
www.nutshellpaints.com
Casein milk paints, herb and resin oils for wood, Swedish floor soap and other natural goodies

LIZ INDUNI

17 Kings Road East, Swanage
Dorset BH19 1ER
Induni@hotmail.co.uk
Limewash

OSTERMANN & SCHEIWE

Unit 2, Pembroke Road
Stocklake Industrial Estate
Aylesbury, Buckinghamshire
HP20 1DB, tel 01296 481220
www.osmouk.com
Natural external and internal wood finishes (as used by Neil Winder); also timber floors

fabrics

CATH KIDSTON

28-32 Shelton Street, London
WC2H 9JE, tel 020 7836 4803
www.cathkidston.co.uk
Fifties inspired fabrics and wallpapers for new retro interiors.

IAN MANKIN

109 Regents Park Road
London NW1 8UR
tel 020 7722 0997
The original saviour of utility fabrics. Reasonably priced plains, stripes and checks

THE NATURAL FABRIC CO

PO Box 163, Banbury, Oxon
OX15 6ZX, tel 01295 730064
www.naturalfabriccompany.com
Range of fabrics including ticking, calico and voile

RUSSELL & CHAPPLE

68 Drury Lane, London WC2
5SP, tel 020 7836 7521
www.russellandchapple.co.uk

Calico, cotton duck, artists' canvas and linen

WHALEYS LTD

Harris Court, Great Horton
Bradford, West Yorkshire BD7
4EQ, tel 01274 576718
www.whaleys-bradford.ltd.uk
Huge range of natural and bleached fabrics - calico. muslin, silk, linen - at reasonable prices

floor and wall coverings

BILL AMBERG

21-22 Chepstow Corner,
London W2 4XE
tel 020 7727 3560
www.billamberg.com
Interior leather - floors, walls etc

BURLINGTON SLATE

Cavendish House, Kirkby-in-
Furness, Cumbria LA17 7UN
tel 01229 889661
www.burlingtonstone.co.uk
Natural slate

BERNARD DRU OAK

Bickham Manor, Timberscombe
Minehead, Somerset TA24 7UA
tel 01643 841312
www.oakfloor.co.uk
Locally sourced oak floorboards

CHRISTOPHER FARR

6 Burnsall Street, London
SW3 3ST, tel 020 7349 0888
www.cfarr.co.uk
Fab modern rugs

SOURCES

LASSCO FLOORING
Lassco Brunswick House
30 Wandsworth Road, London
SW8 2LG, tel 020 7394 2100
www.lassco.co.uk
*Recycled timber floors, from the
humblest to grandest origins*

ROGER OATES DESIGN
The Long Barn, Eastnor
Ledbury, Hertfordshire HR8
1EL, tel 01531 631611
www.rogeroates.com
*Rugs and runners in flatweave
wool, abaca, linen, cotton and
coir in subtly coloured
contemporary stripes*

STONE AGE
Unit 3, Parsons Green Depot
Parsons Green Lane, London
SW6 4HH, tel 020 7384 9090
www.stone-age.co.uk
*Specialists in limestone and
sandstone floors*

STONELL
100-105 Victoria Crescent
Burton-on-Trent, Staffs
DE14 2QF, tel 0800 832283
www.stonell.co.uk
*Limestone, slate and other
natural stone tiles*

one-stop shops

THE CONRAN SHOP
Michelin House, 81 Fulham
Road, London SW3 6RD
tel 020 75897401
www.conran.co.uk

*Modern furniture and
accessories with soul.*

DESIGNERS GUILD
267-277 Kings Road, London
SW3 5EN, tel 020 7243 7300
www.designersguild.com
*Fabrics, furniture and accessories
for town styles with their hearts
in the country*

HEAL'S
196 Tottenham Court Road
London W1P 9LD
tel 020 7636 1666
www.heals.co.uk
*Furniture and accessories with
impeccable design credentials.*

HABITAT
Nationwide stores
tel 0845 601 0740
*Regularly updated range of
quirky accessories and well
designed furniture*

retro furniture

AFTER NOAH
121 Upper Street, London
N1 1QP, tel 020 7359 4281
www.afternoah.com
*A stylishly eclectic shop, with
another branch in Chelsea,
selling a mixture of old and
new furniture and accessories;
strong on new utility style*

MARGARET HOWELL
34 Wigmore Street, London
W1U 2RS, tel 020 7009 9009

www.margarethowell.co.uk
*Alongside her timeless British
clothes, Margaret Howell sells
reissues of Ercol chairs from the
1950s and other reconditioned
postwar furniture, plus pale
turquoise anglepoises and
Robert Welch tableware.*

CENTURY
68 Marylebone High Street
London W1M 3AQ
tel 020 7487 5100
*Specialists in mid-century
Modern American furniture,
also British 1950s*

DAVID GILL
60 Fulham Road, London
SW3 6HH, tel 020 7589 5946
*Uber-smart designer pieces from
the Thirties to present day*

TOM TOM
42 New Compton Street
London WC2H 8DA
tel 020 7288 1996
www.tomtomshop.co.uk
*Post war art and design –
strong on 'Pop ' furniture*

TWENTIETH CENTURY DESIGN LTD
274 Upper Street, London N1
2UA, tel 020 7288 1996
www.twentytwentyone.com
*Design classics from the
post-war period.*

heating

CVO
4 Beaumont Square, Durham
Way South, Aycliffe Industrial
Park, Newton Aycliffe
County Durham DL5 6SW
tel 01325 327 221
www.cvo.co.uk
*Huge choice of slick modern
and post-minimalist fireplaces
and firebowls.*

THE CERAMIC STOVE COMPANY
4 Earl Street, Oxford OX2 0JA
tel 01865 245077
www.ceramicstove.com
*Ceramic wood-burning stoves
built on site - see Neil Winder's
house (see p 90)*

SCAN
www.krog-iversen.dk
*Danish wood-burning stoves, as
used by Philip Hooper (see p58).
See website for UK dealers*

THE CAST IRON RECLAMATION COMPANY
The Courtyard, Preston Court
Farm, Bookham, Surrey KT23
4EF, tel 0208 977 5977
www.perfect-irony.com
*Interesting selection of reclaimed
cast iron radiators*

ARCHITECTS AND DESIGNERS

The work of the following architects and designers has been featured in this book:

BRIT ANDRESEN

9 Ormond Terrace, Indooroopilly

Queensland 4068, Australia

tel 073 878 5855

(see pages 142-143)

JO CREPAIN

Vlaanderenstraat 6,

2000 Antwerp, Belgium.

tel 03 213 6161

Mail@jocrepain.be

www.jocrepain.com

(see pages 20-21, 38-39,

122-123)

MICHAEL FORMICA INC.

95 Christopher Street, New

York, New York 10014, USA

tel 001 212 620 0655

www.michaelformica.com

designer (see pages 68-69)

RICHARD GLUCKMAN

Gluckman Mayner Architects

250 Hudson Street, New York,

New York 10013, USA

tel 001 212 925 8967

www.gluckmanmayner.com

(see pages 68-69)

COWPER GRIFFITH ASSOCIATES

15 High Street, Whittlesford,

Cambridge, CB2 4LT.

tel 01223 835998

www.cowpergriffith.co.uk

(see pages 48-49)

PHILIP HOOPER

Sibyl Colefax & John Fowler

39 Brook Street, London W1K 4JE

tel 020 7493 2231

(see pages 58-61)

ANTHONY HUDSON

Hudston Architects, 49-59 Old

Street, London EC1V 9HX

tel 020 7490 3411

www.hudsonarchitects.co.uk

(see pages 118, 146-147)

CHRISTIAN LIAIGRE

122 rue de Grenelle, Paris

France, 75007

tel 00 33 14 556 1642

(see pages 10, 14-15, 44-45,

64-65, 98-99, 128)

JACQUELINE MORABITO

42 rue Yves Klein, 06480 La

Calle-sur-loup, France.

tel 04 93 32 64 91

(see pages 18, 32, 37)

CLAUDIO SILVESTRIN

Claudio Silvestrin Architects

Unit 412 Kingswharf,

301 Kingsland Road,

London E8 4DS

tel 020 7275 7515

www.claudiosilvestrin.com

(see pages 50-51, 134, 139)

BROOKES STACEY RANDALL

16 Winchester Walk

London SE1 9AQ

tel 020 7403 0707

www.bsr-architects.com

(see pages 150-151)

KATERINA TSIGARIDA

N P Votsi 3, 54625 Thessaloniki,

Greece

(see pages 108-109 above, 116)

NEIL WINDER

Star Yard, Millway Lane, Palgrave,

Diss, Norfolk IP22 1AD

yel 01603 455633

(see pages 90-91, 126, 130-131)

PICTURE CREDITS

The publisher thanks the photographers and organisations for their kind permission to reproduce the following photographs in this book:

BIBLIOGRAPHY

A Pattern Language: Towns, Buildings and Construction, Alexander, Christopher, and others. Oxford University Press, New York, 1977.

The Poetics of Space, Bachelard, Gaston. Beacon Press, Boston, 1969. Paperback edition, Beacon Press, Boston, 1994.

How Buildings Learn: What Happens After They Are Built,

Brand, Stewart. Viking, London, 1994. Paperback edition, Phoenix, London, 1997.

The English House, Muthesius, Hermann. Crosby, Lockwood, Staples, London, 1979.

A Place of My Own: The Education of an Amateur Builder, Pollan, Michael. Bloomsbury Publishing, London, 1997;

paperback edition, 1998.

English Country Houses, Sackville-West, Vita. Collins, London, 1941. Reprinted by Prion, London, 1996.

Landscape and Memory, Schama, Simon. Harper Collins, London, 1995. Paperback edition, Fontana, 1996.

Walden and Civil Disobedience, Thoreau, Henry David. Penguin, Harmondsworth, 1986.

INDEX

A

adobe, 79
Alexander, Christopher, 95, 137, 153
American houses, 136
Arts and Crafts style, 115
attitude, 53-71
Australia, 80, 143

B

Bachelard, Gaston, 104
Baggy House, Devon, 146-7
Belgium, 21
Bertoia, 68
Brand, Stewart, 35, 66, 78, 96, 109, 113, 114
brickwork, 114
Brittany, 64

C

Castle Drogo, Devon, 34
Chelsea, 62
concrete, 113-14, 122
Conran, Terence, 57, 61
corrugated iron, 85
cottages ornés, 67

D

Danish Modern style, 115
Day, Lucienne, 62
Day, Robin, 61, 62

E

European houses, 136

F

fabrics, 115
fires, 31
Foster, Norman, 74

G

Gibbings, Robsjohn, 68
glass, 136-7, 150

H

harmony, 133-53
honesty, 12, 93-111
Hooper, Philip, 56-7, 61
Hudson, Anthony, 146

I

Indiana, Robert, 31

J

Jacobsen, Arne, 41, 129
Jones, Owen, 13
Judd, Donald, 37

L

landscape, 135-53
leather, 115, 121
Liaigre, Christian, 7, 64
linen, 115, 121
log cabins, 12
Long Island, 68
Lutyens, Edwin, 34

M

Majorca, 139
materials, 113-31
metal, 122
minimalism, 33-51
Muthesius, Hermann, 46

N

new rustic style, 73-91
nostalgia, 55-6, 59

P

picture windows, 136-7
Poiret, Paul, 13
Pollan, Michael, 115, 131, 135-6, 137, 145
Poole Pottery, 61
Prairie Houses, 136

R

Renaissance, 115

retro style, 55-71
Rogers, Richard, 74
Romantic movement, 136
rustic style, 73-91

S

Sackville West, Vita, 13, 19, 136
Seventies style, 56
'shackology', 74, 75
Shropshire, 107
Silvestrin, Claudio, 139
simplicity, 9-31
Sixties style, 56, 68
soft furnishings, 115
softwoods, 75, 127
South Africa, 85
Spira, Rupert, 96-7, 107
spirit of country, 11-31
stencilling, 97, 107
stone, 114, 116-19
Stradbroke Island, 143
Suffolk, 127
Sussex, 56-7

T

terraces, 137
Thoreau, Henry David, 12, 34, 45, 136, 140

V

Venini, 61
verandahs, 137, 149

W

Winder, Neil, 74-5
windows, 136-7, 139
wood, 35, 74-5, 115, 127-31, 143
Wordsworth, William, 114
Worthington, Greville, 37
Wright, Frank Lloyd, 136

Y

Yorkshire, 41, 128

AUTHOR'S ACKNOWLEDGEMENTS

I know it is customary to thank one's mother for giving birth and Baudelaire for simply existing, not to mention husband, kids, and the kitchen sink. But I shall stick to the professionals, all of whom are proof that it is possible to be just that – professional – without losing your sense of humour. There should really be three names on the cover of this book, for it would never have happened without the guidance and tenacity of Anne Furniss and the inspired art direction of Helen Lewis. Thanks also to Nadine Bazar, our brilliant and indefatigable picture researcher, and to Rachel Gibson at Quadrille; also to Mary Davies for her sensitive and knowledgeable editing of my text. Andrew Wood – who has such a great eye – took what I consider to be the best photographs in the book. And for that I must also express my gratitude to the owners who opened their doors so hospitably to us townies: Greville and Sophie Worthington, Neil Winder, Rupert and Caroline Spira, and Philip Hooper. Hopefully, Philip has now reflected further on the fact that his house is actually much better suited to me than it is to him; all I ask is that he leave it to me in his will and then take one of those outward-bound adventure vacations up Mount Everest. And finally, though Baudelaire, I'm sure, would have been a tremendous inspiration had I read him, he was absolutely no help at all in looking after my children and washing the kitchen floor while I was writing this book. Kelly Smith was.

This edition first published in 2005 by
Quadrille Publishing Limited
Alhambra House
27-31 Charing Cross Road
London WC2H 0LS

© Text Dinah Hall 1998
© Design and layout Quadrille Publishing Limited 1998

British Library Cataloguing in Publication Data
A catalogue record for this book is available from the British Library

ISBN 1 84400 228 4

Printed China